You At The Back

ROGER McGOUGH

You At The Back

Selected Poems 1967–1987
Volume Two

JONATHAN CAPE
LONDON

Copyright © Roger McGough 1991

First published in 1991 by Jonathan Cape Ltd
20 Vauxhall Bridge Road, London SW1V 2SA

The following collections were first published by Jonathan Cape ©
Roger McGough; *Watchwords*, 1969; *After the Merrymaking*, 1971; *Gig*,
1973; *In the Glassroom*, 1976; *Holiday on Death Row*, 1979; *Waving at
Trains*, 1982.

The Mersey Sound, 1967, and *Melting into the Foreground*, 1986 were
first published by Penguin Books Ltd; *Sporting Relations*, 1974 was
first published by Eyre Methuen Ltd; *Nailing the Shadow*, 1987 was
first published by Viking Kestrel. All are © Roger McGough.

Typeset in Palatino by ᴬ⃥Tek Art Ltd, Addiscombe, Croydon, Surrey
Printed and bound in Great Britain by Mackays of Chatham PLC,
Chatham, Kent.

British Library Cataloguing in Publication Data is available

ISBN 0 224 03111 2

For Hilary McGough

Today, a Real Live Poet will be visiting the School. You at the back, what did I just say?

It begins to go wrong as soon as I enter the building and announce myself to the School Secretary. She has obviously never heard of me and assumes I've come for the job of assistant caretaker.

I remember the name of the Head of English who has invited me. He's taking a class and would I wait in the corridor. So I sit outside the Headmaster's office with the day's delinquents: 14 year olds twice my size who smirk and grow spots before my very eyes. One by one we move along. My palms are sweating now. Will I get the chance to explain to the Headmaster who I am and what I'm doing here? I doubt it, at the speed at which he's stamping out villainy. Will I get detention? Perhaps they still use the cane here. Will I burst into tears after the third stroke and spend the rest of the day blubbering? Luckily I'm saved by the bell. The Head of English arrives in time to whisk me off to the staffroom for a quick coffee.

'Sit anywhere,' he says cheerfully. I lower myself into the nearest armchair.

'Except there.' Suddenly it has become electrified.

'Mrs Johnson.'

'Sorry?'

'Geography.'

'I see.'

Over a scalding beaker of Gnatscafe he tells me that the 6th Form are great fans of my work and I begin to relax, seeing myself in the library with a score of young intellectuals: bright-eyed girls and shy young men eager to explore the jewel-encrusted caverns of my soul. However, they are far too busy studying for A'Levels to see me and so a visit to 4N has been arranged instead.

'They hate school and everything about it,' he enthuses, 'especially poetry, so we think 90 minutes with them might do the trick.'

Do the trick? I wish I could do a trick right there in the staffroom. A disappearing trick. Instead, I am led down the corridor like the tame seal I am about to become.

In every group exposed to a live practitioner of an art it has been encouraged to embrace and has therefore rejected, there are two girls. They usually sit stage left and chew. The Head of English revs up the class with tales of The Scaffold (who?) and refers to poems I wish had never written (and occasionally haven't). He then leaves me to it, locking the door behind him.

I enter the ring and throw in a poem. The two girls glance at each other, throw their eyes to the ceiling like old hats, and chew. They continue to chew in rhythm against me. Synchronised, robotic, and my task is to catch them off guard and to separate them. On a good day I succeed. One suddenly smiles, the other stops chewing. Now each is alone and listening. Having mentally prised them apart and let the poems win them over, the rest of the class is easy. Even the Mike Tyson look-alike stops biting the metal pieces off his desk and removes his Walkman headphones. At the end of the reading the kids applaud, ask questions about how much I earn and where I buy my shoes. The bell goes and I walk out into the sunlight, a free man.

Contents

You At The Back

Goodbat Nightman

God bless all policemen
and fighters of crime,
May thieves go to jail
for a very long time.

They've had a hard day
helping clean up the town,
Now they hang from the mantelpiece
both upside down.

A glass of warm blood
and then straight up the stairs,
Batman and Robin
are saying their prayers.

* * *

They've locked all the doors
and they've put out the bat,
Put on their batjamas
(They like doing that)

They've filled their batwater-bottles
made their batbeds,
With two springy battresses
for sleepy batheads.

They're closing red eyes
and they're counting black sheep,
Batman and Robin
are falling asleep.

Watchwords

watch the words

watch words

the watchword

is watch

words are

sly as boots

takeyoureyesoffthemforaminute

and

all   over

the

away

and   place

up

they're

Assass   in

there is an assass
in the house
hold me tight
hold me tight
hold me and my shad
oh love will surely
find a way out
side a policeman
disguised as an owl
snuggles down in the old oak
not giving a hoot
and dreams of policewomen
disguised as mice

in the tooth

with love
give me your hand
some stranger
is fiction
than truth

without love
I'm justa has
been away
too long
in the tooth

Poem about the sun slinking off and pinning up a notice

---

the sun
hasn't got me fooled
not for a minute
just when
you're beginning to believe
that   grass is green
and   skies are blue
and   colour is king
hey   ding a ding ding
and
     a
         host
            of
               other
                    golden
                         etceteras
before you know where you are
he's slunk off somewhere
and pinned up a notice saying:

MOON

The Fight of the year

'And there goes the bell for the third month
and Winter comes out of its corner looking groggy
Spring leads with a left to the head
followed by a sharp right to the body
    daffodils
    primroses
    crocuses
    snowdrops
    lilacs
    violets
    pussywillow
Winter can't take much more punishment
and Spring shows no signs of tiring
    tadpoles
    squirrels
    baalambs
    badgers
    bunny rabbits
    mad march hares
    horses and hounds
Spring is merciless
Winter won't go the full twelve rounds
    bobtail clouds
    scallywaggy winds
    the sun
    a pavement artist
    in every town
A left to the chin
and Winter's down!

tomatoes
radish
cucumber
onions
beetroot
celery
and any
amount
of lettuce
for dinner
Winter's out for the count
Spring is the winner!'

Poem for the opening of Christ The King Cathedral, Liverpool

O Lord on thy new Liverpool address
let no bombs fall
Gather not relics in the attic
nor dust in the hall
But daily may a thousand friends
who want to chat just call

Let it not be a showroom
for wouldbe good Catholics
or worse:
a museum
a shrine
a concrete hearse
But let it be a place
Where lovers meet after work
for kind words and kisses
Where dockers go of a Saturday night
to get away from the missus
Tramps let kip there through till morning
kids let rip there every evening

Let us pray there
heads held high
arms to the sky
not afraid and kneeling
let Koppites
teach us how to sing
God's 'Top of the Pops' with feeling

After visiting you
may trafficwardens let noisy parkers off
and policemen dance on the beat
Barrowmen knock a shilling off
exatheists sing in the street

And let the cathedral laugh
Even show its teeth
And if it must wear the cassock of dignity
then let's glimpse the jeans beneath

O Lord on thy new Liverpool address
let no bombs fall
Keep always a light in the window
a welcome mat in the hall
That it may be a home sweet
home from home for all.

Storm

They're at it again
the wind and the rain
It all started
when the wind
took the window
by the collar
and shook it
with all its might
Then the rain
butted in
What a din
they'll be at it all night
Serves them right
if they go home in the morning
and the sky won't let them in

Flying

from the ground
one sees only the dag end of clouds
those bits of the blanket
tucked under

Flying
one sees across the counterpane
rumpled, morning white,
as if the earth had spent
another restless night

Bucket

everyevening after tea
grandad would take his bucket for a walk

An empty bucket

When i asked him why
he said because it was easier to carry
than a full one

grandad had
an answer
for everything

Railings

towards the end of his tether
grandad
at the drop of a hat
would paint the railings

overnight
we became famous
allover the neighbourhood
for our smart railings

(and our dirty hats)

Uncle Harry

Uncle Harry was a widower
wouldn't have it anyother way
wore two pairs of socks all year round
with a prayer started each day:

'Oh God, let it be a coronary
something quick and clean
I've always been fastidious
and death can be obscene.

So if today You've put me down
then it's Your will and I'm not scared
but could it be at home please
not where I'll look absurd,

like on the street, at the match,
in the toilet on a train
(and preferably a one off
in the heart and not the brain)'

Uncle Harry was a vegetarian
until the other day
collapsed on his way to the Health Food Store,
rushed to hospital, died on the way.

You may get the vote at eighteen, but you're born with a price on your head

blue sierra
daguerreoscape
echo   echo
in some moonfilled canyon
as a rattlesnake
tosses in its sleep

Time to move on
I kick out the fire
and put my ear to the ground.

He's still there
getting nearer year by year.
The Bountyhunter
who knows my price
closing in.
White bones gleaming like dice
high heel boots
dusty
as sin

There are fascists

there are
fascists
pretending
to be
humanitarians

like
cannibals
on a health kick
eating only
vegetarians

P.C. Plod at the pillar box

It's snowing out
streets are thiefproof
A wind that blows
straight up yer nose
no messin
A night
not fit to be seen with a dog
out . . . in . . .

On the corner
P.C. Plod (brave as a mountain lion)
passes the time of night
with a pillar box
'What's 7 times 8 minus 56?'
he asked mathematically
The pillar box was silent for a moment
and then said
nothing
'Right first time'
said the snowcapped cop
and slouched off towards Bethlehem
Avenue.

P.C. Plod versus
the Dale St Dog strangler

For several months
Liverpool was held in the grip of fear
by a dogstrangler most devilish,
who roamed the streets after dark
looking for strays. Finding one
he would tickle it seductively
about the body to gain its confidence,
then lead it down a deserted backstreet
where he would strangle the poor brute.
Hardly a night passed without somebody's
faithful fourlegged friend being dispatched
to that Golden Kennel in the sky.

> *The public were warned,*
> *At the very first sign*
> *of anything suspicious*
> *ring Canine-nine-nine.*

Nine o'clock on the evening of January 11th
sees P.C. Plod on the corner
of Dale Street and Sir Thomas Street
disguised as a Welsh collie.
It is part of a daring plan to apprehend the strangler.
For though it is a wet and moonless night,
Plod is cheered in the knowledge
that the whole of the Liverpool City Constabulary
is on the beat that night disguised as dogs.
Not ten minutes earlier, a pekinese
(Policewoman Hodges)
had scampered past on her way to Clayton Square.

For Plod, the night passed uneventfully
and so in the morning he was horrified to learn
that no less than fourteen policemen and policewomen
had been tickled and strangled during the night.

> The public were horrified
> The Commissioner aghast
> Something had to be done
> And fast.

P.C. Plod (wise as a brace of owls)
met the challenge magnificently
and submitted an idea so startling in its vision
so audacious in its conception
that the Commissioner gasped
before ordering all dogs in the city
to be thereinafter disguised as fuzz.
The plan worked
and the dogstrangler was heard of no more.

> Cops and mongrels
> like P.C.s in a pod
> To a grateful public
> Plod was God.

So next time you're up in Liverpool
take a closer look
at that policeman on pointduty
he might well be a copper spaniel.

P.C. Plod in Love

Sergeant Lerge put down his knife and fork
and turning to Plod, said
'Yummyyummyyummy, yummyyummy yum yum'
and began to lick his lips.
'Stop licking my lips' said Plod
and moved further down the table.
The Sergeant apologized.
'I'm sorry Constable, . . . forgot myself for the minute
a bad habit I got into at the Police College'
and muttering something
about the way the light from the canteen window
brought a magical softness to Plod's cheeks
he stood up and flustered his way out.
Plod, his appetite gone,
pushed away the remains of his sultana pud
and went into a brown study.
Five minutes later there was a knock
on the study door.
'Come' said Plod.
In came the lovely Policewoman Hodges.
'Sorry to disturb you Constable,
but I believe I left my handbag
on the chair behind you.'
Plod stood to let her pass
and as she did
he felt her serge with pleasure.
This was his opportunity
The moment he'd been waiting for
for ages '. . . er I was wondering . . . er . . . if . . . er . . .
I have a spare ticket for the policemen's ball
next Saturday . . . and . . . er . . . I . . .'
He stumbled over the words.

W.P.C. Hodges helped him gently to his feet.
'I'd love to come with you' she purred
'I'll meet you in O'Connors Tavern at 20.00 hours.'
Plod watched her disappear through the doorway
and feeling that no one man
deserved such happiness
and unable to contain the emotion
made his way downstairs to the bridewell
where, in the loneliness of an empty cell
wept, till the tears ran down his tunic.

P.C. Plod versus the Park Road Rapist

'Hello, Hello, Hello'
thought P.C. Plod
(cunning as a pack of foxes)
'the man sitting opposite me
here in this typical cosy cafe
is identikal to the identikit
picture of the Park Road Rapist.'

Plod mentioned the coincidence
and they both agreed
the resemblance was uncanny
So over a pot of tea
they discussed the case
crime in general
and Everton's chances of winning the Cup.

Eventually
the man looked at his watch
thanked the kindly copper for the tea
and leaving the typical cosy cafe
headed for Park Road.

On the Road

BIRMINGHAM

Auschwitz with H and C
Seven a.m. and vacuum cleaners
at full throttle. Brum Brum Brum.
Grey curtains against a grey sky
Wall to wall linoleum and the
ashtray nailed to the mantelpiece.

At 10. o'clock the Kommodante
(a thin spinster, prim as shrapnel)
balls me out of bed. 'Get up
or I'll fetch the police. Got guests
arriving at midday. Businessmen.
This rooms to be cleaned and ready.'
    (Kleenextissues to be uncrumpled and ironed
    Dust reassembled
    Fresh nail in the ashtray
    Harpic down the plughole
    Beds to be seen and not aired.)

In the lounge my fellow refugees
are cowering together for warmth.
𝔑o gas fires allowed before 6.30
in the evening. Verboten.
We draw straws. The loser
rings the service bell. 'Tea! Tea!!
I've got more to do than run round
making tea at all hours of the day.

Tea!!!' She goosesteps down the hall.
A strange quirk of feet.
When the bill comes there is included
a 12½% service charge.
We tell her to stick it up her brum.

HUDDERSFIELD

Monster cooling towers stand guard
lest the town takes to the hills,
4 p.m. and the sky the colour of frozen lard.

Secondhand soap in my little B. and B.
My only comfort, the Kozeeglow hotwaterbottle,
provided free of charge by the management
after November 15. 'Any chance
of a cup of tea and a sandwich?'
The landlord, senses a troublemaker:
'Breads run out.' I consider following it.

Later, having not taken Huddersfield Polytechnic
by storm, we retire to the Punjab
to lick our wounds and dangle our disappointment
in the curry. Chicken with 2 chapatis.
Home cooking. The real McCoy sahib.

Outside, no one on the tundrastreets
save we eternal action seekers.
Too full to drink, too cold to laugh.
At one a.m. we give up the ghost
town and steam back to the gaff.

in bed I wear socks and my grey woolly hat,
shiver, and regret not having filled the Kozeeglow
with vindaloo.

No. 12 a long room built under the eaves. Tri-
angular. Like living in a giant Toblerone packet.
One-bar electric fire and a meter only takes
threepenny bits. Sore throat and a cold a comin
sure as eggs is eggs is eggs.
Somewhere between here and London
the van has broken down. No band.
No props. It's going to be a fun show
at the Barry Memorial Hall.
'Drink Brains' says the advert on a beermat.
They'd drink anything down here.
Must be the coaldust and all that
choirpractise. Outside its raining oldwomen
and walkingsticks. The pillow feels damp.
Tears of the previous paying guest.
The eskimos in the room next door
speak fluent welsh at the tops
of their voices. Not a drink to be had
T.B. or not T.B. that is the question.
Pneumonia at least. Sure as eggs
is eggs is eggs is eggs is eggs
is eggs is eggs is eggs is eggs
is eggs croeso is eggs is eggs
is eggs is eggs is eggs is eggs
is eggs is eggs is eggs is eggs

BRADFORD

Saris billow in the wind like dhows off the shore
bus drivers whistle ragas above the traffic roar.
Late afternoon, and darkness already
elbowing its way through the crowded streets.
The pavements glister and are cold.
A lady, brittle with age, teeters along,
keeping balance with a shopping bag
in one hand and a giant box of cornflakes
in the other. Lovers arminarm home
to hot soup and a bath-for-two
Everyone a passer-by or a passer-through.

Up at the university lectures are over for the day,
and students, ruddy
with learning, race back to the digs
to plan revolutions to end revolutions.

When asked why he had elected
to pursue mathematics in academic
seclusion, the old prof had answered:
'because there's safety in numbers.'

The occasional curry

keeps

the

stomach

on

its

toes

humdinger

there's not a one

                                      no one

                                  anywhere/place

quite like you

i would follow you to the very ends
of our street

                              and often do

           (discreet-
          ly)

                                onallfours

youra   HUMDINGER

Why, everybody says so

what i wouldn't give for an excursion into your darkest africa.

exsomnia

in bed
counting sheep
my attention
distracted by
a passing nude
when suddenly
a hoof
caught me
on the head
with a soft moan I collapsed

now i lie
by the bed
side more dead
than alive
waiting for the
somnambulance
to arrive

ofa sunday

ofa sunday
the only thing
i burn
at both ends
is my bacon.
Like the tele
phone i am
off the hook

i watch the
newspapers for
hours & browse
through T.V.
miss mass
and wonder
if mass
misses me

bravado

and you still havent ironed
the trousers of my s.s. uni
form. The baby you say
will grow to love a new
father. Someone will come
and do my job properly.
Someone not closed.

beneath the sheets
i pick my nails
and flick
dirtpellets
soundlessly
into the darkness.
Bravado.

vampire

Blood is an acquired taste
'tis warm and sickly
and sticks to the teeth
a surfeit makes me puke.
i judge my victims as a connoisseur
a sip here, a mouthful there.
i never kill
and am careful to cause no pain
to those who sleeping nourish me
and calling once i never call again.

So if one morning you awake,
stretch, and remember
dark dreams of
                    falling
                    falling
if your neck is sore
a mark that wasn't there the night before
be not afeared 'tis but a sign
i give thee thanks
i have drunk thy wine.

warlock poems

when i fly
i keepclose
to chimneystacks and
gutted warehouses
hovering

just out of
reach of men's anger
i take off
from bombed-
sites and model
my tech-
nique on litter
caught

in

the

wind.
(During the day i camouflage myself
to blend against a thousand backgrounds ,
all grey)

my fear
is that one morn-
ing when i have landed
to re-
fuel with sadness
They
will capture me
tie my wings
behind my back
and drive a stake through my fuselage

on a clear night
some
stoned home re-
turner hearing a
cry, might gaze
upwards and see
me silhouett-
ed against the sky
trying vain
ly to get out
through the circular silver escape hatch

i saw
     the hearse
          coming towards me
    it was
       too late
           to turn   back
       when it
           drew level
              the coffin

shuddered
    and the bearers
       had greatest
   difficulty in keeping
         it under control
       the crowd
         turned
         and saw me hiding

they pointed
    and shouted
       and screamed
   everything
      was black
        and purple
     except
       the white faces
          advancing

i took to the air

The Most Unforgettable Character I have ever met gives Advice to the Young Poet

GIVE POETRY A BAD NAME
May your poems run away from home
and live between the lines
May they break and enter, assault and batter
and loiter in the mind with intent
May they invite the critics for dinner
and leave before the main course
May they put a hand up the muses' skirt
(only to find Robert Graves' hand already there)
May the dying be anointed with them
and the living vaccinated against them
May they walk in our sleep
and talk while we are talking

WHEN ASKED TO DEFINE POETRY,
QUOTE THE ONE ABOUT THE ICEBERG
May your poems run riots
and sit outside courts where justice has grown flabby
May they stick in the craw of the law
and fly in the face of gifthorses
May they bushwack bandwagons
then take to the hills
May they pull new tongues at old hats
and milk sacred cows
May they pocket grudges
and compliment unadorned ugliness
May they turn back after its too late

CREEP UP ON POETRY
WHILE SHE'S FEEDING THE DUCKS
May your poems save us
Save us from those who peddle pornography
and who are not sensual
Save us from those who would replace God
with an autographed picture of themselves
Save us from those who think they should lead
because they have followers
Save us from those who think they should lead
because they *want* followers
Save us from those who think they are right
Save us from those who think *you* are right

WHEN POETRY SCREAMS AT YOU
THREATEN TO TAKE UP PAINTING
May your poems act their rage
and cry out against the wilderness you have chosen
May they spit blood into the wind
and once written, seldom regain consciousness
May they brandish themselves in the dark
like a blindman's stick
May they be seen and heard
May they ask the unaskable
Question the unquestionable
May they ring from the rafters
Live happy ever afters
May they be damned, and published.

the power of poets

the man on the veranda
outside, giving coppers
to the old tramp and
feeling good isn't me.
I am the veranda.
I could have been
the tramp or even
the coppers. However
I choose to be the
veranda and it is
my poem. Such is
the power of poets.

Sporting Relations

Big Arth from Penarth
was a forward and a half.
Though built like a peninsula
with muscles like pink slagheaps
and a face like a cheese grater
he was as graceful and fast
as a greased cheetah.

A giraffe in the lineout
a rhino in the pack
he never passed forward
when he should have passed back
and once in possession
s l a a l o m e d his way
through the opposition.

And delicate?
Once for a lark
at Cardiff Arms Park
Big Arth
converted a softboiled egg
from the halfway line.

No doubt about it,
he was one of the best players in the second team.

Uncle Malcolm
put the shot
for Scotland.

When he retired
he collected shots
as a hobby.

At the time
of his death
he had nearly 200

And in accordance
with his last wishes
they were buried with him

at St Giles cemetery in Perth.
Uncle Mal is now at rest
somewhere near the centre of the earth.

Uncle Jed
Durham bred
raced pigeons
for money.

He died
a poor man
however

as the pigeons
were invariably
too quick for him.

Aunt Agatha
blooded at five
loves to hunt foxes
and eat them alive.
No horsewoman
she prefers to run
with the hounds.

On all fours
shod in running-
gloves and shoes
no dog can match her
and once on the scent
nose smell-bent
no horse can catch her.

And she snaps
and she barks
and she urges the pack
onward on
to her bushy-tailed snack.

Tongue flapping
huntingpink suit
nostrils aflare
beware any hare
caught napping
en route.

And she snaps
and she barks
and she urges the pack
onward on
to her bushy-tailed snack.

D'ye ken Aunt Agatha
in her coat so gay
D'ye ken Aunt Agatha
at the close of day
Houndsurrounded
Tearing into foxflesh.

Cousin Chas,
an expert in the art
of self-defence,
would go out of his way
to defend himself.

'In dis age of
senseless violence'
he would explain,
'one must be
equipped to meet
de aggressor
on his own grounds.'
He drank barley wine and guinness
and never bought rounds.

Every Saturdaynight
after a few pints
Chas and his mates
would roam the streets
looking for pale young men
against whom
they would defend themselves.

Cousin Chas
may not have been
one of Nature's gentlemen
but he was a right bastard.

Jennifer Chubb-Challoner
the Cheltenham Ladies
Triple Jump Champion

was first spotted
by a peepingtom talentscout
while still at Junior School

when she won
the 3-legged race
all on her own.

Uncle Jason, an ace in the Royal Flying Corps
grew up and old into a terrible borps.
He'd take off from tables to play the Great Worps
stretch out his arms and crash to the florps.

His sister, an exSister (now rich) of the Porps,
would rorps forps morps: 'Encorps! Encorps!'

Aunt Ermintrude
was determined to
swim across the Channel.
Each week she'd
practise in the bath
encostumèd in flannel.

The tap end
was Cap Gris Nez
the slippy slopes
were Dover. She'd
doggypaddle up and down
vaselined all over.

After 18 months, Aunt Erm was in peak condition.
So, one cold grey morning in March
she boarded the Channel steamer at Dover
went straight to her cabin
climbed into the bath
and urged on by a few well-wishers,
Aunt Ermintrude, completely nude
swam all the way to France.
Vive la tante!

Albert Robinson
(a half-cousin by marriage)
is probably the only
bullfighter in Birmingham.

At five in the afternoon
he parades round the Bull Ring
in his Suit of Lights
(an army battledress
and panty tights
sequinned plimsolls
and padded flies)
a faraway look
in his faraway eyes.

For he struts beneath
Andalusian skies
as concrete corridors
echo the cries
of aficionados
in shoppers' disguise
'El Robbo, El Robbo el mas valiente matador!'

On his way to the hostel
he stops and he buys
a carton of milk
and two meat pies
then it's olé to bed
and olé to rise.

Uncle Trevor and Aunty Renée
won the Northamptonshire
ballroom dancing championship
seven times on the foxtrot.

Practice makes perfect.
Every night after saying their prayers
they glide round the bedroom
for hours on end.

(The nightdress Aunty Renée
wears, she made herself
out of 250 yards
of floral winceyette.)

Uncle Trevor however,
made of sterner stuff
to's and fro'ze
in the buff.

Uncle Terry was a skydiver.
He liked best
the earth spread out beneath him
like a springcleaned counterpane.
The wind his safety net.

He free fell every day
and liked it so much
he decided to stay.
And they say he's still there
sunbathing in the air.

He sleeps each night
tucked up in moonlight
wakes at dawn
and chases clouds.

Living   off   the   food   birds   bring

Uncle   Terry   on   the   wing

Away   from   it   all

Dizzy   with   joy.

Cousin Daisy's
favourite sport
was standing
on streetcorners.

She contracted
with ease
a funny disease.
Notwithstanding.

Cousin Nell
married a frogman
in the hope
that one day
he would turn into
a handsome prince.

Instead he turned into
a sewage pipe
near Gravesend
and was never seen again.

Conversation on a Train

I'm Shirley, she's Mary.
We're from Swansea
(if there was a horse there
it'd be a one-horse town
but there isn't even that).
We're going to Blackpool
Just the week. A bit late I know
But then there's the Illuminations
Isn't there? No, never been before.
Paris last year. Didn't like it.
Too expensive and nothing there really.

Dirty old train isn't it?
And not even a running buffet.
Packet of crisps would do
Change at Crewe
Probably have to wait hours
For the connection, and these cases
Are bloody heavy.
And those porters only want tipping.
Reminds you of Paris that does
Tip tip tip all the time.
Think you're made of money over there.

Toy factory, and Mary works in a shop.
Grocers. Oh it's not bad
Mind you the money's terrible.
Where are you from now?
Oh aye, diya know The Beatles then?
Liar!
And what do you do for a living?
You don't say.
Diya hear that Mary?
Well I hope you don't go home
And write a bloody poem about us.

Smithereens

I spend my days
collecting smithereens.
I find them on buses
in department stores
and on busy pavements.

At restaurant tables
I pick up the leftovers
of polite conversation
At railway stations
the tearful debris
of parting lovers.

I pocket my eavesdroppings
and store them away.
I make things out of them.
Nice things, sometimes.
Sometimes odd, like this.

I say   I say   I say

I say   I say   I say
A funny thing happened on my way here today
The buildings had hiccoughs, the road ran away
Buses grew hair in the silliest places
Traffic lights chuckled and pulled funny faces
3-legged lampposts chased little dogs
The moon took a hiding from stars wearing clogs
Policemen threw helmets at innocent stones
As cheeky boys laughed and broke words with bones
The towns in a tizzy, gone out of its head
Its making me dizzy (I'm going back to bed)

I wish I were a crotchet

I wish I were a crotchet
I'd sing and dance and play
among the dotted minims
all the livelong day

I'd swing from stave to stave
up and down I'd climb
Then crawl from bar to bar
singing all the time

I wish I were a crotchet
or a semi-breve
I'd find a lady quaver
and her I'd never leave

We'd run around the manuscript
a pair of little ravers
get married pianissimo
and raise lots of semi-quavers

Apostrophe

'twould be nice to be
an apostrophe
floating
above an s
hovering
like a paper kite
in between the its
eavesdropping, tiptoeing
high above the thats
an inky comet
spiralling
the highest tossed
of hats

Wink

I took 40 winks
yesterday afternoon
and another 40 today.
In fact I get through
about 280 winks a week.
Which is about 14,560
winks a year.
(The way I'm going on
I'll end up looking like a wink.)

Autumn Poem

litter

    is

        turning

           brown

              and

                the

                  road

                    above

                  is

              filled

            with

          hitch

        hikers

      heading

   south

Slow Paces

slow paces

cloud

patches of sky

cat chases

swallows

catches a fly

          slow paces

          patches

          of cloud in the sky

          cat chases

          catches

          swallows a fly

Rainymorning

the sky
is pretty mad about something
and i don't blame it.
Thats no weather to be out in.
                              Out in
the yard that pretends its a garden
the green bits buckle
under the downslaught.

After the rain
come the violins.
Bluebells
shake their tiny heads in disbelief
Birds
come out of hiding
sing the first song of morning
then fly off to the motorway

to watch motorists queueingt^{oP}i_{leup}

Postcard Poems

i

Iceflow sighted
off Newquay
and they're surfing
in the High Street.
It's women and children first
in the T.V. lounge
and at lunchtime
there was an oilslick
in my soup
'Having a wonderful time
Wish you were her'

ii

Its olé
to bed
and olé
to rise
only the tourists
outnumber the flies

Science, where are you?

I started smoking young. The Big C
didn't scare me. By the time
I was old enough to get it,
Science would have found the cure.
'Ad astra per angina' was the
family motto, and thrombosis
an heirloom I didn't care to inherit.
But I didn't worry. By the time
I was old enough to face it
St Science would surely have
slain that particular dragon.

Suddenly I'm old enough . . .
Science, where are you Science?
What have you been doing
all these years? Were you playing
out when you should have been
doing your homework? Daydreaming
in class when you should
have been paying attention?
Have you been wasting your time
and worse still, wasting mine?

When you left school did you
write scripts for 'Tomorrow's World'
before being seduced by a starlet
from a soap ad? Lured by the
bright lights of commercialism
did you invent screwtop bottles,
self-adhesive wallpaper, nonstick
pans, chocolate that melts
in the mouth not the hands?

Kingsize fags, tea-leaves in bags
beers, bras, voracious cars,
beans, jeans, washing-machines.
You name it, we buy it.

The Arts I expected nothing from.
Good company when they're sober
but totally unreliable. But
Science, I expected more from you.
A bit dull perhaps, but steady.
Plodding, but getting there in the end.
Now the end limps into view
and where are you? Cultivating
cosmic pastures new? Biting off
more Space than you can chew?
Science you're needed here, come down
and stay. I've got this funny pain
and it won't go awa
                           a
                        a
                           a

                             g
                               g
                                 g
                                   h
                                     h
                                       h

Mad Ad

A Madison Avenue whizzkid
thought it a disgrace
That no one had exploited
the possibilities in space
Discussed it with a client
who agreed and very soon
A thousand miles of neontubing
were transported to the moon.

Now no one can ignore it
the product's selling fine
The night they turned the moon
into a Coca-Cola sign.

Newsflash

In a dawn raid
early this morning
Gendarmes arrested
a family of four
found bathing
on a secluded beach
outside Swansea

Later in the day
tracker dogs
led German police officers
to the scene of a picnic
near Brighton.
Salmonpaste sandwiches
and a thermos of tea
were discovered.
The picnickers however
escaped.

The Language of the Rain

You stand behind the curtain
your ear to the windowpane
Listening for secrets
in the chatter of the rain

which clouds got married
which ones left his wife
which winds joined the army
which ones lost its life

You love the latest scandals
you never miss a word
And when the raindrops go away
you write down all you've heard

which mountain keeps a mistress
which ones growing old
which flowers pregnant
which ones got a cold

You keep a little yellow book
and when the windows rattle
You eavesdrop and you then record
nature's tittle-tattle.

which trees bought a new dress
which ones looking pale
which rivers ran away to sea
which ones gone to jail

One night I took your yellow book
and tried to read in vain
For who but you can understand
the language of the rain?

Near to You

America's the land of milk and honey
Australia's healthy and continually sunny
The living in Sweden is clean and sleek
The food in France is gastronomique

Japan's got geishas and the fastest train
China's got noodles and chicken chow mein
India can boast the Taj Mahal
Singapore is a shopping mall

Africa looks to a future exciting
Spain is fandango with wine and bullfighting
Eskimos are tough and used to roughing
Turkey is full of chestnut stuffing

The Belgians invented the Brussels sprout
Germans lieben lederhosen und sauerkraut
Greece abounds in classical ruins
Russian violinists play the loveliest tuins

In Bermuda it's sunny beaches and foam
In Switzerland it's gnome sweet gnome
Italian girls make a di fantastic lovers
Danes are mustard under the covers

From old Hawaii to New Nepal
Foreigners seem to have it all
So if everything abroad is as good as they say
Why do we Britons in Britain stay?

The answer is (and I'm sure it's true)
That all of us want to be near to you

Kyrie

There was a porter
who had ideas
high above his railway station
always causing righteous indignation

he wanted to be
giant amongst men
saviour come again to earth
but his teachings only met with mirth

one bright winters morn
packed in his job
believed the world needed him
dedicated his life to fighting sin

the second day out
crossing the road
apparently in Stockport town
a diesel lorry swerved and knocked him down

back at the station
all the porters
wore mourning masks on their faces
and all agreed he should have stuck to cases

Footy Poem

I'm an ordinary feller six days of the week
But Saturday turn into a football freak.
I'm a schizofanatic, sad but it's true
One half of me's red, and the other half's blue.

I can't make me mind up which team to support
Whether to lean to starboard or port
I'd be bisexual if I had time for sex
Cos it's Goodison one week and Anfield the next.

But the worst time of all is Derby day
One half of me's at home and the other's away
So I get down there early all ready for battle
With me rainbow scarf and me two-tone rattle.

And I'm shouting for Liverpool, the Reds can't lose
'Come on de Everton' – 'Gerrin dere Blues'
'Give it to   *' – 'Worra puddin'
'King of der Kop' – All of a sudden – Wop!
'Goal!' – 'Offside!'

And after the match as I walk back alone
It's argue, argue all the way home
Some nights when I'm drunk I've even let fly
An given meself a poke in the eye.

But in front of the fire watchin' 'Match of the Day'
Tired but happy, I look at it this way:
Part of me's lost and part of me's won
I've had twice the heartaches – but I've had twice the fun.

* Insert name of Anfield hero.

Cupboard Love

Recoin some phrases
to sing your praises
but you don't want to know

touch your arm
say what's the harm
but you just want to go

you're unbending
no happyending
you make your way to the door

(things could be worse
I've pinched your purse
it's with all the rest in the drawer)

Estate

Mother!
They're building a towncentre in the bedroom
A carpark in the lounge, it's a sin.

There's a block of flats going up in the toilet
What a shocking estate we are in.

Chicken

Some nights
when I've had a few
I ask the world
to take off its coat
and step outside.
Luckily for you
it's always chickened out.

A Good Poem

I like a good poem
one with lots of fighting
in it. Blood, and the
clanging of armour.   Poems

against Scotland are good,
and poems that defeat
the French with crossbows.
I don't like poems that

aren't about anything.
Sonnets are wet and
a waste of time.
Also poems that don't

know how to rhyme.
If I was a poem
I'd play football and
get picked for England.

Streemin

Im in the botom streme
Which meens Im not brigth
dont like reading
cant hardly write

but all these divishns
arnt reely fair
look at the cemtery
no streemin there

Another brick in the wall

'Its like bashing your head against a brick wall'
said the teacher,
bashing my head against a brick wall.

Nooligan

I'm a nooligan
dont give a toss
in our class
I'm the boss
(well, one of them)

I'm a nooligan
got a nard 'ead
step out of line
and youre dead
(well, bleedin)

I'm a nooligan
I spray me name
all over town
footballs me game
(well, watchin)

I'm a nooligan
violence is fun
gonna be a nassassin
or a nired gun
(well, a soldier)

Bestlooking Girl

I'm the bestlooking girl in our year
It's a fact

All the lads fancy me, and the girls
Are jealous

Mind you, all the lads here are rubbish
Just like kids

My boyfriend is a deejay in town
In a club

He sounds american but he's not
He's scottish

He wants to get on Radio One
Then TV

He thinks I'm sixteen so I let him
Now and then

Out and About, the Lads

pants flapping round legpoles
like denim flags

necks open to the wind
their element

boots the colour of raw liver
boss the pavement

out and about
the lads

voices raised like fists
tattooed with curses

outnumbered rivals
they take in their stride

lampposts and pillarboxes
step aside

out and about
the lads

thick as thieves
and every one a star

Paul uses a knife
you dont feel a thing

Des the best speller
the aerosol king

out and about
the lads

cornered young
they will live their lives in corners

umpteenagers
out on a spree

looking for the likes
of you and me

out and about
the lads.

The Lesson

A poem that raises the question:
Should there be capital punishment in schools?

Chaos ruled OK in the classroom
as bravely the teacher walked in
the nooligans ignored him
his voice was lost in the din

'The theme for today is violence
and homework will be set
I'm going to teach you a lesson
one that you'll never forget'

He picked on a boy who was shouting
and throttled him then and there
then garrotted the girl behind him
(the one with grotty hair)

Then sword in hand he hacked his way
between the chattering rows
'First come, first severed' he declared
'fingers, feet, or toes'

He threw the sword at a latecomer
it struck with deadly aim
then pulling out a shotgun
he continued with his game

The first blast cleared the backrow
(where those who skive hang out)
they collapsed like rubber dinghies
when the plugs pulled out

'Please may I leave the room sir?'
a trembling vandal enquired
'Of course you may' said teacher
put the gun to his temple and fired

The Head popped a head round the doorway
to see why a din was being made
nodded understandingly
then tossed in a grenade

And when the ammo was well spent
with blood on every chair
Silence shuffled forward
with its hands up in the air

The teacher surveyed the carnage
the dying and the dead
He waggled a finger severely
'Now let that be a lesson' he said

Tide and time

My Aunty Jean
was no mean hortihorologist.
For my fifteenth birthday
she gave me a floral wristwatch.
Wormproof and self-weeding,
its tick was as soft
as a butterfly on tiptoe.

All summer long
I sniffed happily the passing hours.
Until late September
when, forgetting to take it off
before bathing at New Brighton,
the tide washed time away.

Contact lenses

Somenights
she leaves them in
until after they have made love.
She likes to see clearly
the lines and curves of bodies.
To watch his eyes, his mouth.
Somenights she enjoys that.

Othernights
when taken by the mood
she takes them out before
and abandons herself
to her blurred stranger.
Other senses compete to compensate.
Without lenses, blindly accepts her fate.

Funny sort of bloke

Have you heard the latest scandal
About 80-year-old Mr Brown?
He stole from Matron's handbag
Then hitchhiked into town.

Had a slap-up meal at the Wimpy
Then went to a film matinée
One of them sexy blue ones
We're not supposed to see.

Then he bought some jeans and a toupee
Spent the night in a pub
Then carried on till the early hours
Dancing in a club.

They caught him in the morning
Trying to board the London train
He tried to fight them off
But he's back here once again.

They asked him if he'd be a good boy
He said he'd rather not
So they gave him a nice injection
And tied him up in his cot.

He died that very night
Apparently a stroke.
Kept screaming: 'Come out Death and fight.'
Funny sort of bloke.

Missed

out of work
divorced
usually pissed

he aimed
low in life
and
      missed.

Vegetarians

Vegetarians are cruel, unthinking people.
Everybody knows that a carrot screams when grated.
That a peach bleeds when torn apart.
Do you believe an orange insensitive
to thumbs gouging out its flesh?
That tomatoes spill their brains painlessly?
Potatoes, skinned alive and boiled,
the soil's little lobsters.
Don't tell me it doesn't hurt
when peas are ripped from the scrotum,
the hide flayed off sprouts,
cabbage shredded, onions beheaded.

Throw in the trowel
and lay down the hoe.
Mow no more
Let my people go!

W.P.C. Marjorie Cox

W.P.C. Marjorie Cox
brave as a lion
bright as an ox
is above all else, a girl.
Large of bosom
soft of curl.

Keeps in her dainty vanity case
diamanté handcuffs, trimmed with lace,
a golden whistle, a silken hanky,
a photograph of a popstar manqué
(signed: 'To Marjorie, with love'),
a truncheon in a velvet glove.

W.P.C. Marjorie Cox
cute as a panda
in bobby sox.
Men queue to loiter with intent
for the pleasure of an hour spent
in her sweet custody.

Vague Impressions

Ossie Edwards couldn't punch a hole in a wet echo.
He was no fighter.
And if he wasn't thicker than two short planks
he wasn't much brighter.
To compensate, he did impressions.
Impressions of trains, impressions of planes,
of James Cagney and Donald Duck.

As they all sounded the same
his impressions made little impression
on the 3rd year Cosa Nostra
and so he was bullied mercifully.

Then, quite suddenly, Ossie saw the light.
One Monday morning during R.I.
he switched to birdcalls.
Peewits, kestrels, tomtits and kingfishers
he became them all.
Larks and nightingales.
The birdnotes burst from his throat
like a host of golden buckshot.

And as the nearest anyone got to ornithology
was playing football on a debris with a dead pigeon
there could be no argument.
So he was rechristened 'Percy'
and left alone.
And left alone
he twittered his way happily to 3 'o' levels
and a job in a shipping office.

'Twas there he met Sylvia
whom he courted and married.
She took an interest in his hobby
and they were soon appearing in local concerts:
'The Sylvatones – Bird Impressionists'.
The double-act ended however
when Sylvia left him for a widower
who taught her how to sing.
Her love for Perce she realised
never was the real thing,
but, like his impressions, a tuneful imitation.

And that was years ago and still
whenever I pass that way at night
and hear the shrill
yearning hoot of an owl,
I imagine Percy
perched out there in the darkness,
lonely, obsessed.
Calling for his love
to return to the nest.

An Apology

Owing to an increase
in the cost of printing
this poem will be less
than the normal length.

In the face of continued
economic crises, strikes,
unemployment and V.A.T.
it offers no solutions.

Moreover, because of
a recent work-to-rule
imposed by the poet
it doesn't even rhyme.

Two Haiku

only trouble with
Japanese haiku is that
you write one, and then

only seventeen
syllables later you want
to write another

Limerick

There was a young lady from Dingle,
Who liked music that made her all tingle,
And she really did rave,
About the song of the cave,
(you know, the Mendelssohn one about Fingal).

Rainbow

With a rainbow under your arm
you came a-calling.

A home-made cardboard cut-out.
A spangled boomerang. A gift.

That night we put it on the bed.
Made love, a wish, and slept.

(Later, your rainbows would appear
in bedrooms allover town)

With a rainbow under your arm
you came a-calling.

A two-dimensional cartoon of the real thing.
Tongue-in-sky. Our love.

Shy

The shy girl at the party
turned out to be

the shy girl in the car
turned out to be

the shy girl in the bedroom
turned out to be

with the light
turned out to be

shyning!

Scintillate

I have outlived
my youthfulness
so a quiet life for me

where once
I used to
scintillate

now I sin
till ten
past three.

The Battle of Bedford Square

At a publishing party in Bedford Square
The critic is at ease
With lots of lady novelists
To flatter and to tease

He's witty, irresistible,
Completely on the ball
A few more wines, who knows,
He might make love to them all

But one by one they disappear
With a smile, and a promise to phone
And suddenly it's midnight
And suddenly he's alone

He surveys the litter, arty,
In search of a back to stab
Anger jangling inside him
Like an undigested kebab

Across the ashen carpet
He staggers, glass in hand
And corners a northern poet
Whose verses he can't stand

As if a bell had sounded
A space had quickly cleared
They were in a clinch and fighting
And the waiters, how they cheered

There was a flurry of books and mss
Bruises on the waxen fruit
A right to a left-over agent
Blood on the publisher's suit

A hook to a Booker Prize runner-up
A left to a right-wing hack
A straight to the heart of the matter
And the critic's on his back

An uppercut to an uppercrust diarist
From an anthropologist, pissed,
An Art Editor's head in collision
With a Marketing Manager's fist

Two novelists gay, were soon in the fray
Exchanging blow for blow
As the battle seeped into the Square
Like a bloodstain into snow

And though, at last, the police arrived
They didn't intervene
'What a way to launch a book.
Bloody typical Bloomsbury scene!'

All that now of course is history
And people come from far and wide
To see the spot where literary
Giants fought and died

Holding cross-shaped paper bookmarks
They mouth a silent prayer
In memory of those who fell
At the Battle of Bedford Square.

Is My Team Playing
(after A.E. Housman)

Is my team playing
That I used to cheer
Each Saturday on the terrace
Before I transferred here?

Aye the lads still battle
They go from strength to strength
Won the FA cup
Since you were laid at length.

Is factory still closed
With pickets at the gate?
Would I could lend a hand
Ere I felt the hand of Fate.

No things are back to normal
Thanks to the TUC
Our wages now are frozen
But not so much as thee.

And my lonely widow
Does she nightly grieve
For her dear departed
Gone early to the grave?

No she's right as rain
And not the one to weep
She is well looked after
Be still my lad, and sleep.

And what of you, dear friend
Are you still unwed
Or have you found a lady
To share your bachelor bed?

I said, dear friend, I said
Have you found a lady
To share your bachelor bed?
Hello . . . Hello . . . Anybody there? . . . hello . . . hello

The Scarecrow

The scarecrow is a scarey crow
Who guards a private patch
Waiting for a trespassing
Little girl to snatch

Spitting soil into her mouth
His twiggy fingers scratch
Pulls her down on to the ground
As circling birdies watch

Drags her to his hidey-hole
And opens up the hatch
Throws her to the crawlies
Then double locks the latch

The scarecrow is a scarey crow
Always out to catch
Juicy bits of compost
To feed his cabbage patch

So don't go where the scarecrows are
Don't go there, Don't go there
Don't go where the scarecrows are
Don't go, Don't go . . .

Don't go where the scarecrows are
Don't go there, Don't go there
Don't go where the scarecrows are
Don't go . . . Don't go . . .

Don't go where the scarecrows are
Don't go there, Don't go there

I Don't Like the Poems

I don't like the poems they're making me write
I really don't like them at all
Hierograffiti I don't understand
Scrawled on a hologrammed wall.

They wake me up in the middle of the night
I really don't like them one bit
Dictating mysterious messages
That I am forced to transmit.

Messages with strange metaphors, ass-
onance, similes and the like.
Internal rhymes that chime, and alas
External ones that sometimes don't quite make it.

I don't like the poems they filter through me
Using words I never would use
Like 'filter', 'hierograffiti', 'alien'
I'm enslaved by an alien muse.

* * *

And I notice, just lately, at readings
That friends whose work I have known
Unknowingly have started to write
In a similarly haunted tone.
Stumbling over poems we have to recite
In handwriting that isn't our own.

low jinks

today
i will play low jinks,
be commonplace

will merge,
blend, change
not one jot

be beige, behave
my friend
will fault me not

couching myself
in low terms
i will understate

holding
my breath
until nightfall

i will be
neither seen
nor heard

it will be
exactly the same
as yesterday

when
nobody noticed
nobody cared.

For Want of a Better Title

The Countess
when the Count passed away

During a Bach
cello recital

Married an Archduke
the following day

For want of a better title.

Green Piece

Show me a salad
    and I'll show you a sneeze
Anything green
    makes me weak at the knees
On St Patrick's day
    I stay home and wheeze
I have hay fever all the year round.

Broken-down lawnmowers
    Bring me out in a sweat
A still-life of flowers,
    in oils, and I get
All the sodden signs
    of a sinus upset
I have hay fever all the year round.

A chorus of birdsong
    makes my flesh creep
I dream of a picnic
    and scratch in my sleep
Counting pollen
    instead of sheep
I have hay fever all the year round.

Summertime's great
    (except for the sun)
Holly and mistletoe
    make my nose run
Autumn leaves and I swoon
    it's no fun
Having hay fever all the year round.

Conservation Piece

The countryside must be preserved!
(Preferably miles away from me.)
Neat hectares of the stuff reserved
For those in need of flower or tree.

I'll make do with landscape painting
Film documentaries on TV.
And when I need to escape, panting,
Then open-mouthed I'll head for the sea.

Let others stroll and take their leisure,
In grasses wade up to their knees,
For I derive no earthly pleasure
From the green green rash that makes me sneeze.

Trees Cannot Name the Seasons

Trees cannot name the seasons
Nor flowers tell the time.
But when the sun shines
And they are charged with light,
They take a day-long breath.
What we call 'night'
Is their soft exhalation.

And when joints creak yet again
And the dead skin of leaves falls,
Trees don't complain
Nor mourn the passing of hours.
What we call 'winter'
Is simply hibernation.

And as continuation
Comes to them as no surprise
They feel no need
To divide and itemize.
Nature has never needed reasons
For flowers to tell the time
Or trees put a name to seasons.

Wheelchairs

After a poetry reading in a geriatric hospital

I go home by train
with a cig and a Carly.
Back at the gig
the punters, in bed early
dither between sleep and pain:
'Who were those people?
What were they talking?'

The staff,
thankful for the break,
the cultural intrusion,
wheel out the sherry
and pies. Look forward
to a merry Christmas
and another year of caring
without scrutiny.

Mutiny!
In a corner,
the wheelchairs,
vacated now, are cooling.
In the privacy of darkness
and drying piss,
sullen-backed,
alone at last,
they hiss.

Ode on a Danish Lager

The finger
enters the ring. A
pplause. Hooray!
Unzip.   A
pause. Then, whoosh,
The golden spray.

Unfurling slowly
like a blue mist
from a sorcerer's cave,
the genie is released
to serve a master
(soon to be slave).

A sip to mull over
the flavour
found only in the first.
I make a wish,
then slake,
an imaginary thirst.

I squeeze the can
(it is not cannish),
is yielding, unmanish.
In it, my reflection,
modiglianish.

We wink at each other,
We're getting on well,
The genie weaves
his genial spell.

I unmask one more
(unheed the body's warning).
Goodnight, sweet beer,
See you in the morning!

What prevents a poem
from stretching into Infinity?

what prevents a poem
from stretching into Infinity
is the invisible frame
of its self-imposed concinnity

Muffin the Cat

Written at the Arvon Foundation
Lumb Bank, Yorkshire

I had never considered cats
until Nadia said I should:
'If a person likes a cat,
then that person must be nice.'
So I seized the chance to be good
by taking her advice.

When Muffin (not the mule) called
around midnight to inspect the room
I was, at first, distinctly cool.
Until, remembering the New Me,
I praised felinity and made tea.
Offered him a biscuit. A cigarette.
Tried to make conversation.
He'd not be drawn. Not beaten yet
I showed him my collection
of Yugoslavian beermats.
He was unimpressed. (Queer, cats.)

At 2 a.m. I got out the whisky.
He turned up his nose.
After a few glasses I told him
about the problems at home.
The job. My soul I laid bare.
And all he did was stare.

Curled up on the duvet
with that cat-like expression.
Not a nod of encouragement.
Not a mew. Imagine the scene;
I felt like that intruder
on the bed with the Queen.

But I soldiered on till morning
and despite his constant yawning
told him what was wrong with the country.
The class system, nuclear disarmament,
the unions, free-range eggs.
I don't know what time he left.
I fell asleep. Woke up at four
With a hangover the size of a Yorkshire Moor.
And my tongue (dare I say it?) furry.

Since then, whenever I see the damn thing
He's away up the mountain to hide.
And I was only being friendly.
I tried, Nadia, I tried.

The Boyhood of Raleigh
After the painting by Millais

Entranced, he listens to salty tales
Of derring-do and giant whales,

Uncharted seas and Spanish gold,
Tempests raging, pirates bold.

And his friend? 'God, I'm bored.
As for Jolly Jack I don't believe a word.

What a way to spend the afternoons –
the stink of fish, and those ghastly pantaloons!'

Laughing, all the way to Bank

The beautiful girl
in the flowing white dress
struggled along the platform
at the Angel.

In one hand
she carried a large suitcase.
In the other, another.

On reaching me
she stopped. Green eyes flashing
like stolen butterflies.

'Would you be so kind
as to carry one for me,'
she asked, 'as far as Bank?'

I laughed: 'My pleasure.'
And it was. Safe from harm,
All the way to Bank,
Moist in my palm, one green eye.

From *Les Pensées* by Le Duc de Maxim

Beside the willowèd river bank
Repose I, still and thinking,
When into the water fall a man
Who fast begin the sinking.

Chance at last to test
A maxim, so unblinking,
I toss to him the straw
Through which I drinking.

Sure enough, he clutch the straw
And scream, alas in vain.
He grasp until he gasp his last
And all is peace again.

Homewardly I pensive trek
Impatient now to note
How the fingers of the sun
Did linger on his throat.

And how he sank, and how
The straw continuèd to float,
'How wise the age-old axioms,
And yet how sad,' I wrote.

Good Old William

'I concur
with everything you say,'
smiled William.

'Oh yes,
I concur with that,
I agree.'

'If that's the general feeling
You can count on me.
Can't say fairer.'

Good old
William, the Concurrer.

Worry

Where would we be without worry?
It helps keep the brain occupied.
Doing doesn't take your mind off things,
I've tried.

Worry is God's gift to the nervous.
Best if kept bottled inside.
I once knew a man who couldn't care less.
He died.

Prayer to Saint Grobianus
The patron saint of coarse people

Intercede for us dear saint we beseech thee
    We fuzzdutties and cullions
    Dunderwhelps and trollybags
    Lobcocks and loobies.

On our behalf seek divine forgiveness for
    We puzzlepates and pigsconces
    Ninnyhammers and humgruffins
    Gossoons and clapperdudgeons.

Have pity on we poor wretched sinners
    We blatherskites and lopdoodles
    Lickspiggots and clinchpoops
    Quibberdicks and Quakebuttocks.

Free us from the sorrows of this world
And grant eternal happiness in the next
    We snollygosters and gundyguts
    Gongoozlers and groutheads
    Ploots, quoobs, lurds and swillbellies.

As it was in the beginning, is now, and ever shall be,
World without end. OK?

A Crocodile in the City

The crocodile said to the cockatoo:
Cockatoo,
A croc's gotta do
What he's gotta do

The crocodile said to the chimpanzee:
Chimpanzee,
I want to be free
The jungle jangles not for me

The crocodile said to the mosquito:
Mosquito,
I must quit, oh,
I must admit, I just must go

The crocodile said to the koala bear:
Koala bear,
What are you doing up there?
ɐᴉlɐɹʇsn∀ uᴉ ǝq plnoɥs no⅄

The crocodile said to the parakeet:
Parakeet,
I'm stifled by this steamy heat
How I long to loll on a stone-cold street

The crocodile said to the alligator:
Alligator,
À l'heure, alligator, mate,
See you at a later date

The crocodile said to the piranha:
Piranha,
I leave for London *mañana*
Disguised as a giant banana

The crocodile said to the hippopotamus:
Sharon,
Give my love to Karen,
Gary, Wayne and Darren

Dear Mother

London cold Earth hard
Buildings giant into sky

To and fro menwo scarry
as if time on fire

At great noise cars speed
trailing bad breath

Crocodile keep to gutter
where slidder undisturbed

Dear Mother

Prisons underground
for rats are many found

Cats and dogs cowed
kowtow to menwo

Birds are not radiant
nor celebrate lives in song

Are pavement-coloured
and scream

Dear Mother

During daylight sightsee See
sights for sore eyes

See eyesores soar
So far have sightseen

Buckingham Palace Tower
Bridge Houses of Parliament

Yesterday went to Madame Tussaud's
and ate lots of famous people

Dear Mother

Night is best Moonlight
become crocodile

Stars dance in scales
asa hunting go

Late home-returner
beware puddle that move

Beware reflection that salivate
Moonlight that become crocodile

Dear Mother

Arched in pain
on pavement

Throat dry
as parchment

Parched
thirst saharan

Water water
sting of carbreath

Dear Mother

London hard Earth cold
Too tired now to hunt meat

Eat Coke cans McDonald's cartons
Kentucky fried chicken boxes

Water is black Like swallowing
putrid snake Cannot see

Tongue is swollen Head is burning
Tomorrow crocodile return home

Kentucky fried snake

Home is cold carton

chicken is swollen water

mother is putrid meat

    earth is dear

    Coke is hard

McDonald's is tired now

    head is black box

    tongue is swallowing

    London is burning

crocodile cannot see

                        tomorrow

Ten Questions I'd Rather Not Answer

i) Why did they nail her shadow to the ground?

ii) Has the mirror seen the last of me?

iii) Out there, are they whispering, or shouting quietly?

iv) If I hit the headlines, will they hit me back?

v) My first memory: in my cot playing with a death rattle?

vi) Why is the sixth one always so difficult?

vii) Words left unsaid, are they sad, do they whither away?

viii) Can the darkness be pacified?

ix) Where do my hands finish?

x) Why is my mouth screaming?

Let me explain . . .

Index of First Lines